The Government of Nature

Pitt Poetry Series

Ed Ochester, EDITOR

The
Government
of Nature

Michael Afaa Weaver

蔚
雅
風

UNIVERSITY OF PITTSBURGH PRESS

Published by the University of Pittsburgh Press, Pittsburgh, Pa., 15260
Copyright © 2013, Michael Afaa Weaver
All rights reserved
Manufactured in the United States of America
Printed on acid-free paper
10 9 8 7 6 5 4 3 2 1

ISBN 13: 978-0-8229-6231-1
ISBN 10: 0-8229-6231-4

for my parents

安心
赤膽忠心
心口如一
心花怒放
心滿意足

平心靜氣
動人心弦
專心致志
心明眼亮

Contents

IV

The Government of Nature

I

Through the course of Nature
muddy water becomes clear . . .

—*Dao De Jing*, chapter 15

Buddha Reveals the Apocalypse to the Cowboy

God is not the author of confusion.
—I Corinthians 14:33

The harness comes tight up under the throat, whistle
caught the way the desert tightens a howl in hot dust
without air, the single hairs on your arm at night the pages
in the book that will write itself in your grave, your bones
turning with the embryo still caught, a peculiar failure
of the body that makes sages weep, no mesh for the night

of death to keep the maggots away, no gathering of prayers
in the loom that moves the veil between here and there,
the gate where bodhisattvas sit to counsel the desperate,
their song something you take as fool's gold, roiling
last chances, throwing them back to the mixing bowl
sitting somewhere in the continuum of space and time.

Your father was his grandfather, the man on the running
board of the 1940 Chevrolet, when America dreamed
its highways, the connection that bound us to desert fruit,
as you built your own ultimatums, no way to see the engine
of what drove you to speak holy names as convenience,
no sense of samadhi, no sense of lying down to let wrong
write itself on the heart's tablet, exorcise this thing in you,
a mutated ambition, you the son of the morning light.

Evening Lounge

after the painting by Brent Lynch

The humid nights are best and worst, best
because the birds sing at two in the morning when
you cannot get back into the other world, worst
because it is the moist heat that makes the skin supple,
makes you want to rub against someone else, a woman,
and there is nothing but the long list of lost chances,
things you could have said, perhaps the simple question
of *will you sleep with me* so that it is not just you
and this shell of a home, this place where it feels
the walls are another layer of my skin, and that is neither
best or worst. It is the holding of the dead stink,
the memories that wash over me, holding them back.

It is the utter singleness of being the only person
here, the way the thoughts think themselves down to
accepting that this is really just me here wondering who I am,
just me here wondering why I am awake at two,
which trigger it was, knowing all the time all too well
the way the war of life is connected to the nervous system
of the world, the ganglia of our shared horrors, either
mine so large, or so people tell me, and here it seems
to be the membrane between the skin of my bones
and the skin of this home, the absorbing shock of space
that gives when the memories burn their way in or
out of me. I would lie here wondering how to tell her
I am wrestling with the angel, wrestling with memories
in the crevices and cracks of my body, of how I feel
right now, what it felt like then, in those times, and I am
glad she is not here, and I wish she were here, and she
has no name because this is some woman I do not know.

I practice in the silence of my thoughts the different pitch
and rhythm of how I might ask *will you sleep with me*,
afraid of what to say should she say *yes* and this decade

4

of my monkish life should lie open and I have to say why
I am sitting on the edge of bed, why I have woke her from
the sweet smile I assume she has when I assume her horror
is smaller than mine.

The Path

Without my umbrella I forget the rain, welcome
each drop to forget me. The stones take more time
to know, their separate grooves and slopes,
different slanting into the light, one face for the moon,
one face for the clouds. In the wetness I hear
honeysuckles tipping over at the edges, a frog
jumping to reach the higher grass, lost somehow.
At the end I put my hand out to touch what love left
for me the last time I came searching, alone.

With the umbrella I stumble, too lonesome
for the way water soaks into the skin in the thunder,
listening for the sound of the eagles circling
above the lost children of wild pigs or what can be
caught and carried in the talon. My hands are
not free, too busy with trying to keep the cover
on my head. The stones have another meditation,
a kind of counting to music. Touch me, they say,
and a thousand stone paths will make their way to me.

Once in the night when it was dry, when the pretty
rain of mountain springtime was suspended,
I walked this path to the dream of where we live.

The Ten Thousand

The rain comes late, draws the afternoon into darkness,
no light where there should be light, no way to be but drenched
until it curves down over your lips. The taste of every living thing
is in the rain drop the way all things open their eyes inside
a single bloom in the garden that is now hushed in a robe.

Whatever you feel about it, whether you live for it or pray
for the rains to die, the water joins with all of us, tendon, bone,
artery, vein, saliva, everything that melts and goes hard, escapes
as air. The water brings a reunion for a moment with what we know
each time we breathe ourselves here or are forced to breathe.

If I write without color it is to obey the gray way rain brings
the past to us. The ten thousand are one giant palace with a room
for remembering, where you must stand alone, touch and believe
while it seems you are touching nothing and have gone all mad
in this life, this gift. We are sitting on a rock in the thick falling

of water, purple lilies are growing in the sun's ocean shadow,
sheep with golden wool are flying in the trees, a patient monkey
is bandaging a wounded blade of grass, the garden is a mesa,
seeds are mountain caves, the moon has gone infinite, made
two of its own selves for each of our palms. Now we have faces.

A Dream of Emptiness

The ecstasy of being eaten is more than the fear
in the teased air between pine needles and red lilacs
where we take turns shooting through the thin circles
made on the edge of the hawk's wings, the tiny space
it cannot come back to except to arc up again,
navigate, draw once more the line from her eye

to a place where we have no escape. It is the way
the heat pumps the whole mountain until it is drunk
with sun, so full of it that its stone heart melts
to make its own waters trickle down the slopes
to gather in the gullies, softening the ground
for the snakes who have lost their envy of dragons.

It is the teeth, sometimes the sweet juice of the mouth,
the belly flesh of the jaws, the eyes falling back
into themselves with relief from hunger. We think
ourselves invisible but still the lure of going in
is greater than the fear of never coming out, so we give
ourselves to the joy of change. Time always ignites

again, even from the great time of nothing that spat
the world from *the long sleep*, that too a hunger
like this way we ache to know desire lives in the eye.

Tsunami

December 26, 2004

Do not rush to know the difference as that will be a door
too large for those who rush. Take instead the slow touch
of bamboo. Come each morning to the same tree and rub
it slowly the way you would rub a limb of your own.
Know that you may lose it to a surgeon's knife and touch
every thin line. Feel the color of a single shaft of the thing
the way you would find the smallest places on a finger.
Put your lips against the leaves the way you would kiss
the hair on your own arms. Embrace it with all of you
and promise to keep the farmer's axe away. Promise to shoo
away the poison air of the cities. Ask the earth to bless
it with children that are bamboo. Come at night and wait
for the bamboo to sing in the wind, wait until the song comes,
until hunger makes you angry. Think of the lines of bamboo,
how they shoot up and then bend with their accomplishment.
This may take more years than you have, or you may press
the bamboo into a heartless fear of its own beauty.
If so, start again, more slowly this time. After each step,
pray for the children who went back into the sea without
enough time to learn the songs of bamboo, or to remember.

Leaves

The lines that make you are infinite, but I count them
every day to hear the stories you carry. These are not secrets
but records, things we should know but ignore. If I commit
the sin of tearing you from the tree, I find another world
inside the torn vein, another lifetime of counting the records
of who walked here before, of what lovers lay here
holding each other through wars and starvation.

Some days I stand here until I lose focus and travel,
drifting off out of the moment, too full of it, and my legs
are now like trees, mindless but vigilant, held
into the earth by the rules of debt, what we owe
to nature for trying to tear ourselves away. I drift
and the pleasure of touch comes again, layers of green
in the mountainside a tickling in my palms.

The pleasure is that of being lost here in the crowd
of trunks and pulp, the ground thick with the death of you,
sinking under my feet as I go, touching one and another,
linking myself through until the place where I entered
is gone. When I am afraid, my breath is caught in my throat.
When I am not afraid, I lift both hands up under a bunch
of you to find the way the world felt on the first day.

Walking with Snakes

The snakes congregate near the garden.
It's what everyone says, and sometimes I forget
when I see the red tree, the one that sits alone
near the vegetable sprouts, across from the pipe
network for the canopy that no longer hangs.
It is the sudden red and the way it changes
in the middle of all the fallen bamboo that now
makes the cracking sound of fallen bamboo.

I forget my walking stick for a moment,
but it does not forget me, always there, too early
a reminder of what help we need when we are older.
But I keep it to pound the ground as I walk
and let the snakes know that I am coming.
It is said that Omo Sango have snakes as their messengers,
but here in the throng of lilies on Buddha's birthday
I should remind them to first ask me for the message.

It is said there is one snake here that will not run
when it hears monks walking, pounding the ground.
Curling, they speak a wire resistance to intruders.
Lost for a moment in the red tree, my walking
stick reminds me where I am, dry bamboo in my hands.

A Monk's Ode to Guan Yin

If there is a cliff in the green of the mountains
take me there, tie me to the edge so I will always
know the gate to the truth. Dangle my feet in the air
so the ambitious worm can stand on its tail, tell me
again how the road goes in places where there are
no maps, no dashboard computers. Leave my food
on a down slope so the fruit and bread roll to me
just when hunger says it is time and there is water enough
to stop the thirst. My hands refuse to grieve.

When they should be palm to palm around a clump
of lilies, they go instead looking for hidden
circles in your waist, the uneven favorite note they know
when they count your accumulations, name the victories,
go sliding all over until there is no line between
palm and you, everything is one body. This side
of the ocean has let go of waves, lies there mimicking
the sky with blue paling away. Wetness is the name
of it, when all I can feel is the craving to feel until

A single car stalls at night, there is a tear in the grass,
and a hawk catches some lost thing rambling alone.

Guan Yin's Treatise on Compassion

At night the garden sleeps and changes itself,
adds new lines to a path, uncovers a small stone well,
moves the shadows of the temple so the sun
must adjust. The temper of the earth changes,
blue is more blue, green is less green, the white
streaks of clouds are thinner smiles. Last night
there was a rainbow working in it all, making
more of what was less, feeding the thick way trees
cover the rough way up the mountain. I am
here at your feet waiting to see how you make
suffering less of what it is, how you take a worn heart
and kiss it over with lips attuned to giving, and
when you move from your perch here, there
will be a chance. I will lean over to where you were
and see all the secrets of getting through, of how
to climb through where leaves are as thick as tears
in the ocean, of how to call the eagles down
to land in my hand and dance without tearing me.

This morning I went out again, walking, despite
the crack in the bone, the slip of gristle in the joint.
In the corner of the gravel road, I found another paradise.

II

What rises up appears bright
What settles down appears dark

—Dao De Jing, chapter 16

Damascus

If we could hear the private noise of my ears
it would be the snap of a twig under his foot,
my parakeets at the wire door of their cage,
my model of Lon Chaney's hunchback beating
Notre Dame's doors, crying for sanctuary,

a crackle in the earphones of the RCA radio
that put me to sleep, drowned the sound of sin,
the velvet of horse muzzle brushing against me,
Grandma's hand covering her son from a wasp
the nights he cried himself into his own anger,

his tiny fists in a pillow under pine whispers,
pounding as if to beat fish to pulp in a barrel,
this sound of forced forgetting, of memories
that refuse to die and slip out into the bloody water
of some bright day with God where he remembers

children bound in suffering must carve their mercy seat,
the blood dripping onto pages of heaven's record.

Flying

A hand pulled me open, down on the bed,
down on the bed, looking up, holding the covers
while the soft soul of me, like a crab's inedible meat,
lifted away, meat with thick strings that hold together,
then elongate themselves to keep me tied,
bound in the body until this lifting, the soul's ugly meat
becoming wings and I flew, above the house, the graves
behind it in Baltimore Cemetery with grandma's
marker holding our names. The ceiling was the law
saying *stop!* . . . until the hand gave me the gift
of flying . . . in my heart, *yes, it is the heart*. Night
became a magnet of my craving to be one thing
forming in the womb of my mother where
nascent nubs of *self* take shape, the brain still
asleep in its mysteries until the heart awakens,
thumps itself into beating with a drum song we know
in the endless connections of intestines and brain,
mind of gut . . . *mind*. Sages say we can fly
when God falls asleep, his arm hitting the floor
we call Earth so *the touched* can dream of home.

If You Tell

If you tell, the stars will turn against you,
you will have not night but emptiness.

If you tell, you will live in an old house
in the desert all alone with cacti for friends.

If you tell, people will hide their children
from the monster others say your kind are.

If you tell, the police will add you to the list
of people who might have killed the albatross.

If you tell, you will walk in a hollow room
full of the sound of *liar, liar, pants on fire.*

If you tell, poets will call it marketing,
a ploy to get ahead in the game.

If you tell, women will think you are trying
to steal a place that is not yours.

If you tell, you will become a stinky thing
no aromatherapy will ever make sweet.

If you tell, all the therapists you ever saw
will claim you in reports to some conference.

If you tell, you will see the wounded everywhere,
shuffling legions, the murdered souls of children

under angels' wings, beating a prayer in a place
with no night, no day, no palladium of lies.

The Ancestors Speak to the Cowboy

Rejoiceth not in iniquity.
—1 Corinthians 13:6

In truth you knew he was yours to teach, to guide,
to know as spirit over the child flesh, to accept
the way we knew each other in worlds before this,
before the shadow made you an apostate,
a rogue disciple, and pine rushes taught you
lies are truth and truth are lies, the killing space
of saints. You sang back to it in baby boy
voices, gave yourself over to the promise that life
is a making, that absolutes are the way to define
the touch, your hand over his eyes when the spirit
moved you, as you told him it was a dream,
that it was special, a map to outside worlds,
countries on the other side of the door, sleeping
into the metamorphosis, a rude betrayal,
he full of your rawness, of transmissions,
long lines of generations recorded on dried bark
somewhere in the beginning of time where
you fell headfirst into some lust, a sadness,
misguided fingers turning pages in prophecies.

Interpretation of Tongues

to the cowboy

What voice speaks to him in the silence,
the empty barns at night, fixing a bridle?

What voice speaks to him without music,
siren in poplar trees, he the mute soldier?

What voice speaks to him from the dead wish
of ambition, driving horse trailers to Ohio?

What voice speaks to him when the crickets come,
sit in his window with millions of blank stares?

What fills arias in his opera of the forgotten,
bodies he once knew by heart, without heart?

What is the harmonic of the whispers
setting his eyes on nymphs and children?

In what precise twist of the inner drum
did he hear mayhem instead of magic?

God, tell us so we can chant the invocation,
collect the proper incense and brass urns,
weave the bright cloth to bind this Satan.

The Ancestors Explain How Envy Grew

Calm appeared, his soul stopped, a crow
staring as he snatched down miniature angels,
trapped them in jars, capping the light away
to make a hush out of glory songs, a crying out
from the joyful aubades they breathe as easy
as moonlight on jars of preserves, their throats
full of fear now, the brave breast crumpled
in his child fingers, their prisons invisible
to the cherubim searching for heaven's missing
songsters trapped in blind ways of getting even
at a world that would make him small, make
him an impotent wonder, curl his genius under
like a witch's toes when his father died
chewing on cheese and cornbread, chocolate
surprise in the sun, an unkind ending.

He grew in the way of genius, no charts
showing where he ended and the world began,
how cities figure in the jagged sweep of cornfields,
endless thousands of shouts up into the evening,
listening to the future speaking, like the old man
in the schoolyard, a stranger by the wishing pond
in the woods, or dogs that stand up like men in hats—
these the Corinthian signs he mistook
for an alphabet giving the right to molest children.
Now wisdom is sour rubbing medicine pasted
over nightmares, not the proper wealth of an old man,
the arms of his neighbors around him like laurels.

Scapegoat

I will hand him this, the blank spaces in knowing
myself, handling the foreign body that is my own in the dark,

reeling in the betrayal of this temple, earth and water,
skin and blood, bone the hard mix that makes me fly away

from what they call sane, and I will hand it to him
in the gentle *mano a mano* that is the way of angry men,

the only gentleness he knows, hard hands on the bridle,
stuffing the metal of the curb bit until the horse's tongue

bleeds like the hands and feet under the nails, or the severed
head of someone who dared practice a faith spelled in books,

this thing, I hand him the weight of years, a single feather
from a man called less than a man by men who do not know men.

Elegy for the Appaloosa's Mother

for the cowboy

The blood bay mare, deep red black with yellow,
her mane in waves after we braided it, white blaze
frosting her nose. I took too long to comb her,
patting her up under her belly the way a fourteen-year-
old boy would do. He snatched the brush away
before I could get to cool her down with water,
snatched her from my hands to his hands,
from the soft wonder to a rough smack
of a backhand as a threat, a backhand that beat
a stallion until the white of its eyes came untied
from the bony back of an eyeball's soft gel.
Fear hit me the way tears light up like flames
afraid to let themselves go when a child is made
to know what animals must know, the beating down,
blood and meat where spirit and song should be.

He bred this mare named after dreaming of names,
bred her to the neighbor's proud Appaloosa stallion—
some blood bay on his front, a big blanket behind,
white spread over his rump with dark dots like eyes,
bred her and brought her back to say the foal was mine,
mine for odd reasons he would not name, we
walking into the farmhouse, through the back door
to the kitchen, telling me he was going to leave me
a million dollars, a million dollars of insurance after
he is gone to the coffin, when all I can do is stroke
the thin fibers of his good hair and the touch of saddle
that skin comes to be, hardness the hollow wood of death,
or the way things are beaten, down, down, until
the hands of hurt force a child to nurse on terror.

Against Forgiveness

In the moonlight the leaves telegraph
the night's song, the way they brush against
us as we go under the wooden bridge
across from the Jesuit seminary, stepping
in streams, the horses tunnels of living flesh
that we trust. My faith in him is absolute.
We go into the woods where mad things
can turn the horses into monsters that maim
and crush, but he holds life up with hands
named by what nature tells the living.

I know it from the shadows of whispers
in my mind, from the earliest games in a space
a big brother should have had but was taken by him,
my uncle like a chocolate bear in the dark,
bear that I keep close to me, carving
a dark father from questions I do not know,
questions I have not the courage to ask
as one asks a question to step from shadow
and become the light that leads, shines
on the words carved in stone by water.

The Government of Nature

Dear body of mine . . .

Rosetta stone of my soul, *familia vascellum*,
I have brought you to the arbor of memories,
in the clinging vines, playing *Negro spirituals*
for parakeets with mouths turned upward,
as we were when we came into the world,
me a sheaf of unwritten contracts, you a chemistry
wrestled out of love and fate, dear body of mine,
organs and nerves, vessels, pineal window
to inner space, the intersections of visions.

What abbreviated paternoster do we summon
in the night when the hand upturns the sacred portion
of a child and mixes the nerves to make monsters,
uses them for what feels unnatural, abridges
and aborts the will, or is it the will itself come down
to the only path that will let us be the difficult unknown
in the calculus that is our test along the way
to forgetting, as we agreed to this, to the pain,
the crying out for mother as trusted hands molest
a child split from the herd to bind it with karma
until the *Dhammapada* nods the way to Nirvana.

I come with you to places I cannot go alone, as alone
I would be only the decision to be, not the things
I cannot explain to anyone, except in the privacy
of a piety I have had to own, a profane saintliness
that came to me in places too foul to remain buried
in me, these places—lotus ponds, mountains, waterfalls,
divine insignia in closets, bedrooms, bathrooms—
these places a carnival I now name as redemption,
sins multiplying, lifting the eyes of cumulus clouds
praying over the urges that rise from memories
of rape, the loneliness kept in *Grace's* silence.

Dear body of mine, I push off from a knowing
that tears my eyes into a steady stream, leaving
the medulla, a tuft of grass on a hill looking up and out
to the wise fool in the center of the mind, as wishes
fall back from the perimeters of the skin, beneath to
the bone, inside the marrow to pierce the centers
of selves until knowing leaves us, tender and mortal,
desire a river longing itself into being, lost in mirrors.

III

My mind is like the autumn moon
clear and bright in a pool of jade.

—Cold Mountain #5

For James

our beloved

Touch his body, a thought said,
but the doors to the parlor of the dead
were closed, the streets empty—

I stood there for an eternal second,
no tears, no inclination, no pulse,
gone into the stone way of dying

with the dead the way grief
sounds itself in our bones, beating
the marrow into stillness.

The Pantry

It's cold and tin that put me back there,
chill places where things are stored, a day
in some autumn, a supermarket where
the colors and smells and even feel of the floor
add up to some convergence in the spirit,
and I hear you, blessed uncle, saying it's time
to play the game again, or even alone
in a park somewhere, open to the whim of chance
that is what our minds are, as our minds
are all of what we are, and here you are
again, inside me, telling me it's time to play
the game again, as if I am not over fifty now,
and do not know that I was hardly the speck
of what this arthritis has come to be, how
high this blood of mine with its pressure
so that all the world's relaxation leaves me
still with medicine I swallow and come
back to the cold and tin of the pantry—you
singing your hypnosis song of how I have
to play this game, how it is time again
to take things I do not want, and yet I know
enough to know it is not candy, and that it could
choke me if I say bad things about it, make
the dragon inside it rise on a tail of fire and
then spit at me again, the spit the awful
that makes me feel unclean until I take
the dragon like some Perseus, count its nine
heads, the nine heads someone gave to you,
and cut them, one by one, until they are
roses, blushing pink, tender to the touch,
and I come back to some faith that innocence
has a more sacred seduction that is one heart
giving itself to another heart, confessions

in the way of chanting saints, things too big
for a little boy needing a hand to knock
you down, set a holy fire in the pantry,
burn it, send it the way of the unclean.

Germany, in the Fifties

You went away, left me, and came back
with a woman, paraded her in front of me
as if this was what I should want to do

when the time came, as if the time had not
already come, the time to know what to do
when the muscle hardens, when it awakens

to what the poets say about spring, the place
where all perfection comes again with promise
like this place I know in the curve of your hand

coaxing me with other promises, contracts
made with sin so that now I watch you
with her, wonder what she has that I don't have.

In the Park with My Grandchildren

Fifty-five years and pages ago, my feet
were the size of the feet of these children,
with white shoes, my mother pressing
the ironed sides of her skirt with hands
worried by too much work, by the failure
of my flat feet, a blame she gives
to the womb, or so I imagine in a daydream
when I should be watching the sky to see
the spiraling of angels tumbling down.

This municipal ground of the ordinary
and spectacular, marked by praise songs
like the vocational high school there,
the cement mousetrap of a place for kids
other children teased, thinking themselves
nonchalant and brilliant, blind to the world
that laughed at our poor, black innocence.
My granddaughter picks up wood chips,
throws them back down to disturb the sleep
of worms and the undead dirt that waits.

I fold my wings in rituals no one can see,
pack them into the vinyl grocery bag
from the supermarket to save trees,
the noise of the day the evenness of what
folk do in this part of the world, cultivating
a humor in the imposition of the poor,
patting the air to mark memories, staring
into empty spaces in the street, doorways
where the undiminished become children.

Remember

for my granddaughter

If I forget to plug the sun,
let me know

If I forget to tame the sharks' teeth,
let me know

If I forget to stop the tsunamis,
let me know

If I forget to tie up the bears,
let me know

If I forget to chase away the viruses,
let me know

If I forget to clean the unclean foods,
let me know

If I forget to stop rushing cars,
let me know

If I forget to tame the lightning,
let me know

If I forget to melt the slippery ice,
let me know

If I forget to outlaw nightmares,
let me know

If I forget to put perverts away,
let me know

If I forget that the divine thing
moved inside me to write this,
the thing that can do all things,
let me know
let me down easy
into the earth.

At Lake Montebello with James

Living just enough, just enough for the city . . .
—Stevie Wonder

It is the shared surface of water that reminds
us of being human, the invisible connectedness
that freezes as one, melts as one, lays itself open
in the sun to be a mirror, one vast or tiny glass.

The articulate embroidery of shame is the curse
of taking breath, leaving out of the infinite space
of spirit to come into this elaborate rhythm
and blues, the precious gifts, the shortcomings.

We must hold the silver thimble on the thumb,
sew, mend our way back over our lives to make
sense of what happened to us, while we both
had to bear this cross, with the gifts of music.

The ecumenical shaft of light comes down
into the car when you start to cry, going back
to what happened to both of us in different places,
the thing that happens to boys everywhere.

Everywhere is the carelessness of God, His
way of letting things slip so that the world will
collapse as it should one day, and then rise
back into a testimony for hope, for life.

I take the steering wheel with both hands,
let the tears accumulate, hold them for private
wailing sessions like the ones I have now,
the lake's joggers jiggling past the window.

Scrapple

It was cousin Alvin who stole the liquor,
slipped down Aunt Mabie's steps on the ice,
fresh from jail for some small crime.
Alvin liked to make us laugh while he took
the liquor or other things we did not see,
in Aunt Mabie's with her floors polished,
wood she polished on her hands and knees
until they were truth itself and slippery
enough to trick you, Aunt Mabie who loved
her Calvert Extra and loved the bright inside
of family, the way we come connected in webs,
born in clusters of promises, dotted
with spots that mark our place in the karma
of good times, good times in the long ribbon
of being colored I learned when colored
had just given way to Negro and Negro was
leaving us because blackness chased it out
of the house, made it slip on the ice, fall
down and spill N-e-g-r-o all over the sidewalk
until we were proud in a new avenue of pride,
as thick as the scrapple on Saturday morning
with King syrup, in the good times, between
the strikes and layoffs at the mills when work
was too slack, and Pop sat around pretending
not to worry, not to let the stream of sweat
he wiped from his head be anything except
the natural way of things, keeping his habits,
the paper in his chair by the window, the radio
with the Orioles, with Earl Weaver the screamer
and Frank Robinson the gentle black man,
keeping his habits, Mama keeping hers,
the WSID gospel in the mornings, dusting
the encyclopedias she got from the A&P,
collecting the secrets of neighbors, holding

marriages together, putting golden silence
on children who took the wrong turns, broke
the laws of getting up and getting down
on your knees. These brittle things we call
memories rise up, like the aroma of scrapple,
beauty and ugliness, life's mix
where the hard and painful things from folk
who know no boundaries live beside
the bright eyes that look into each other,
searching their pupils for paths to prayer.

When My Heart Failed

A top floor in Victorian Philadelphia,
the night sounds the tap and blast of gunfire,
above my landlord and landlady in love
since childhood, the house a tree
itself, the windows sudden spaces in leaves,
roots running down to where there is no
sense of what roots do, under a map's wishes,
a slice of cheesecake at Sam's,
the store with the dog that never moves,
the steps I know by heart, from tree to tree,
cracks in the sidewalks signed by my feet
after a year here, tearing away at strange
feelings and memories. I have come to have
a high noon with the past, to meet the maker
of sadness inside me, and tonight it is
one slice of cheesecake, and no soda.

I hit the sidewalk and feel the feeling
of turning to cement where flesh should be,
trudging instead of walking, my chest full
of some new mix, like a cake batter that needs
more vanilla extract and hot butter, or a throat
jammed with a good-bye, somewhere between
a sigh and a smile. My chest has a diamond
where my heart should be, a puzzle's pieces.

Each tree a rest stop, five minutes to go
fifty steps, and I cannot count because the night
looks like having lived to be a kind of success,
second to what grows in trees without light.

In Raleigh's Brownstone Hotel

A night, sleep too thin to hold me,
out of the crevice in the ceiling,
a crawling sits on the bed next to me,
a voice I know, calling itself memory,
pain in places only rape knows.

In a clump of trees, the woods
near my room, I do *Taiji*, a loud,
difference in this Carolina, this roll
of prayers from dead hands, no one
to see me, to count me as strange,
a black Chinese moving in me.

A Sunday, a car of church folk hits
a wall inches behind me, license plate
saying *I'm Blessed*, missing the chance
to name blank spaces in scriptures
where incest has no language.

On Hearing Beethoven's *Moonlight*

In the tech room, on the tech table, the tech people
all around, one says,
        "Mr. Weaver, good news. The arteries
are clear!"

        "Mr Weaver, bad news. Your left ventricle
is barely working!"

        "Mr. Weaver, you can see your heart on
the monitor!"

Oh glad hour, the saints tiny ballerinas on the glistening
surface of stainless steel, language a river that swallows,
chokes away the thing I think I want to say but cannot,
the song I want to sing.

        "Dr. So and So, good news.
this is MY life, my one good, sad, but brilliant life."

The tiny dancers on the table only I can see say at once . . .
tra la la . . . tra la la . . . tra la la.

My mother takes me inside once more,
and there is nothing no one can give me.

I have decided to be born again, to know
what touched me so I can send it flying.

Looking Up from the Naked Bed

One spring I find myself with a woman,
craving love's raw way, getting high on sex,
thrill of skin and breasts, losing myself,
my medication for my heart failing to slow
my addiction until this door opens, above
what I call love. I see myself, a child,
feel the hands of the man carving
the cross I carry, its totem marks.

It is the season of crows, a sudden flock
takes to the tree outside, landing
on the limbs until the tree is a heart,
a wide bottle tapering to the arteries.
The end of time will be drums stopping
blood's hard duty inside this world, rolling over
into Nirvana, a rhythm like the woman
who put me in the arms of Jacob's angel.

The Touched

He was the neighbor who washed his car
in the rain, in sunshine, on Sundays to spite
the pious, in playtime when our balls hid

under his precious whitewalls, and when
it rained he wore his coat, the old rubber
kind, a balloon with big buckles to match

the buckles on his galoshes, and the gold
of his Cadillac was God's way of lighting
everything around him so he could be safe

from neighbors who called him strange.
The soldier's metal in his head matched
the metal of his car, certified him as our

own crazy black man, our own *cbm*,
one of those people who was touched, who
would do anything, who could snap the way

a branch caves in under snow, we watching
the way children do, not knowing men
who are touched were made to know hard

fingers and probing hands can shape life,
lead them to war's killing fields where souls
who live through the dying come home

to a freedom in dry spaces between rain
drops, unlit eyes of the ignorant counting
every move, blind to what makes saints.

The Untouched

Freed for good this time, quiet rooms
far behind me, filed away with old thoughts
of medicine, dim views of what lay ahead,
I work again on humility in the way
Grandma taught me to crochet, patiently,
looping one stitch to another until a thread
is born like the strings physicists say
make dimensions inside, between us.

I learned to crochet and ignore the world,
bend my thirteen-year-old head down to pay
attention to promises of lovely things
to come at the end of needles and string
so now that is how I know the threads
of things, what comes from faith in hands.

In Good Samaritan Hospital

My father is in the hospice, swimming
down under in the deep tide of strokes,
failing organs, the blossoming of memories
into dreams. I take the elevator on the ground,
see a figure hobbling on a cane to the door,
my uncle, his eyes bright survivors of heart attacks
and back operations, of accidentally shooting
his leg playing quick draw, amusing himself.
I hold the door open so we can ascend.

He has the same way of smiling at a nephew
he has loved in ways he cannot understand.
This is a test, of the elevator, of moldy
accounting books in hands of the judges,
where patient spiders crawl into lamp shades
that light the darkened corners of our lives,
a test of the weight on the cables of this thing,
the switches that move the current into place,
sending invisible messengers to light buttons,
count the floors going up into the throat,
a hollow space in this building, this charity.

We are on the floor, walking together, me
looking to give him space but not so much
that he fall, the arm and cane failing the dance
of joint to helping stick, until we are down
the hallway, a surprise in the air, a surprise
when we turn and my father's failed eye
opens to the bloody space of his ending
to let him know rage will not overtake me,
rob me here where death's rattle is music.

Driving South from Salem

Autumn, 2009

In the slow crawl up the highway, near
the signs for Massachusetts, the road less cruel
than it was the night I drove down from Philly,
my father beside me in his last Chevrolet,
a rain so thick our throats felt full with tongue
the way it is when the woman beside you is more
than you can ever be, and sometimes I think
I am a coward in the heart, and what an unkind
thing to think, after bringing a failed heart
back to life, after meeting my mind's ghosts,
taking them down through the threshing,
a daily act of forgiveness, the one prayer.

It has been a good meeting with a circle
of friends, all of us damaged children inside,
under the facade of adults busy at being grown.
There are signs for places with cheeseburgers,
coffee, muffins at every angle, somewhere
it seems these lines should be more carefully
metered, some anapest for the way night goes,
two soft moves and the moon's silent drum
in the distance, the long stretch that is too far
to walk, our bonds to cars and highways so busy
with this ground to speculate on turning upward
to the moon and still stay in the lines of the lane.

Hushed and still as one blink of an eye asleep
at the wheel, there were no lost chances for me—
this poem that could never have been a sonnet,
the wounds of Baltimore too deep for faces
that want to cast spells on a lyric that had to look
into life's finality and find a reason to laugh.

With My Family at Dinner on Easter Sunday

Stop, in the name of love . . .
            —The Supremes

We are a family with the interweaving of stories,
each one a tailored fit to where we are in life, each
memory its own singular lie in a place where lies
are subverted by the fact of a family dying down
until the young are old, and the old hope the young
are the wise old ones come back to do the tally
of damages not so collateral when a tiny village
goes after the burning of karma's ribbons, each tear
in the fabric an undoing of a soul's thread, the line
that keeps us here, so many pearls scattered in mud.

Judgement is a frugal light in a body of chips
for a nervous system, more like the jagged surrender
of rocks over cliffs than the way we wind into dusk,
the macaroni and cheese, lasagna, chocolate eggs,
all the recipes of narrative that make a people
a ganglia of shared bloods and histories, and I know
this evening with its finality of acceptance is a script
cast when matter took on the arrogance of thought
and we gave IT the names of our gods and dreams
so we can worship ourselves with our own names.

I will not be moved from the pineapple upside down
cake in the midst of everything, each solid settling down
of a memory a settling with hands that know heaven's
underside, the way the floor of the place oppresses
those of us who would think we know why we suffer,
and for the old hands of the one aunt I have left, the one
uncle I have left, their courage I can now know more
than imagine, I hold out my hand to some drunken angel
for my reprimand, for daring disbelieve the nameless
who come down on a one millimeter speck to bless me.

Evensong at Christ Church

In the ceiling is the miracle,
the stone locking to stone, holding
up the place, and when the priest
strides over in his garments, I want
to join the sanctuary, be settled
in the Book of Common Prayer, tied
into the histories of wills to power
inside the single strand of my soul,
be a foreigner visiting the inexact art
of wanting to breathe, wanting to test
the lives between earth and nothing.
Not the unlettered blood or its least
atom of difference move my knees
too stiff to kneel, prayers and tears
edging out of forgotten closets.

Holding the seam of my split self
out into the aisle, I make a wish
no one can see in their chanting,
as I pray over the Messiah's naked
body, our unlikely communion,
to summon the least bloodied atom
of what can be whole again.
In Oxford the evenings are order
to our unordered eyes, the left right
backward origin of English, choirs
of stares when we pause at corners,
the whole place my extended self
turned inside out as a child, spun
into the cruel search for a truth
of what I was intended to be,
my own flesh to my own bones.

Washing the Car with My Father

It is the twilight blue Chevrolet,
four doors with no power but the engine,
whitewall tires, no padding on the dashboard,
the car I drive on dates, park on dark lanes
to ask for a kiss, now my hand goes along
the fender, wiping every spot, the suds
in the bucket, my father standing at the gate,
poor and proud, tall and stout, a wise man,

a man troubled by a son gone missing
in the head, drag racing his only car
at night, traveling with hoodlums to leave
the books for street life, naming mentors
the men who pack guns and knives, a son
gone missing from all the biblical truth,
ten talents, prophecies, burning bushes,
dirty cars washed on Saturday morning.

He tells me not to miss a spot, to open
the hood when I'm done so he can check
the oil, the vital thing like blood, blood
of kinship, blood spilled in the streets
of Baltimore, blood oozing from the soul
of a son walking prodigal paths leading
to gutters. Years later I tell him the stories
of what his brother-in-law did to me, and

he wipes a tear from the corner of his eye,
wraps it in a white handkerchief for church,
walks up the stairs with the aluminum
crutch to scream at the feet of black Jesus
and in these brittle years of his old age we
grow deeper, talk way after midnight,
peeping over the rail of his hospital bed
as we wash the twilight blue Chevrolet.

Petunias

for my mother

The cement border kept them on one side,
on the other bricks pushed down in the lawn
while they outgrew and spilled over the lilies,
far away from my sweet potatoes, the food
from roots I started in glass jars in the window.

You came in the quiet moments, in one of your
old dresses, walking side to side on old slippers
in late spring, days before we built the awning
that made shade where there was no shade,
added the tapping sound of the rain to our ears.

In the rain the petunias held up, the strangeness
of fragile stem and bright petals, the violet inviolate
it seemed, under the rain that fell until the slurping
was like a tongue going up and down some part of me
I will not name here, not on this page, not in this light.

The slurping like the slurping today, here in this place
where I have barricaded myself for ten years, the bars
on the windows, the back wall a solid stack of giant
stone bricks set before *your* mother was born, secure
now, I listen to the rain, how it is kept away from me.

If I choose to walk in it, this glory as natural
as undisturbed sex in undisturbed lives, it will feel
and smell like something welcome, something I want—
had I not been undressed, had I not been handled
in the dark and made to know an evil wetness.

At night I wonder how deep my sleep would be
had you known I was in danger and saved me.

Cold Mountain

It is not the stone or the cave's hollow way
without heat, or the dead stillness in a tiger's eyes
turning to dig razor claws deep into soft flesh

the way death aligns itself with life, none of this
is what Cold Mountain means, leaving the city,
climbing up into the hills to pull time away

from itself. It is the way spirit reveals itself
in the bones, where spirit lives, dances into bright
sparks of electric in the trail it uses to travel

in us with lines that have no map except
what poets make, the dream vision, the film
of mucus over the baby's face, a veil

seeing into our other worlds where allies
root for us, give us a slight chance when we go
up to the wall to sit in silence, to remember

nothing from nothing leaves the rise and falling
away of breath. At Cold Mountain I found dirty
mirrors where I hoped to see my own clean face.

IV

Once you are in harmony with the path, then inside,
outside, and in between are ultimately ungraspable, immediately
empty, yet solid, you are far beyond dependency.

—Ying-an

Passing through Indian Territory

On horseback, I tell them to imagine me on horseback
going back to Boston, an oversized wool overcoat on top
of layers of things that make themselves warm against me,
old tops of boxes of pictures of horses pressed flat
to mesh and weave like cloth, I tell them it might take me
a few months to get home because I like to stop when I travel,
pull over so I can rest, and what about falling asleep
on the horse, what about what I did not imagine, smokestack
man slumped down snoring in a saddle, sliding over
to the edge of the grace of horses, their mercy, forgiveness
even for people who forget how the lines between territories
are made of the flesh of ghosts who had no words for where
land ends or where land begins or why there is a horse
waiting for me to answer for the uncle who killed her.

Predators

A blonde draft horse stomps, then the sudden hush,
the geese, tiny bowls of feathers for hearts, a bliss
gone into stillness, ruling the space into a dead absence
where there can be no air in the promise of storms
against wildfires, or a cat's camouflage, flesh to grass,
its claws tucked in so only softness touches the dirt,
gone invisible the way hunters do, tiny as they are
against the urge of trees and bends in the river, no hope
here and no hope of knowing, or is it we who know
nothing of what is play, what is abandon, how much
a day depends on bringing home twice our weight,
big as we are, and so we drive up the path, watch both
sides of the barn's blind spot for drivers who cannot
see us waiting, slowing the breath to take this chance
to move into the perfect lay of field and trees, some
natural order, a brushstroke along an endless breath.

Weeping Willow

> That which goes against the Dao comes to an early end.
> —Laozi

Eyelashes on the breeze, up under it,
bristling like the peacock, the trunk
a hand sitting on its wrist, rooted and bound
in the earth, in our wishes, the ice cream truck
just a horn honk and bell away, down the street,
vanilla and chocolate, mixed or separate, cones
or cups, banana splits when we were rich
with somebody hitting the number in the street,
my mother counting the coins in her hands,
telling the driver to wait at the curb for us,
hand signals from the porch while we climbed
down from this tree of peeping eyes, unruly
in the way nature orders things to be, we climbed
from safety to be the thing the willow kept
from us, the world and all its dangers, a mother
too full with ache to guard her children, leaning
on them in some wrong ways, passing the pain
from one soul to another, forgetting the songs
that can show us the way to knowing.

1963

It was the pair of light blue pants from Sears
that smelled like petroleum, the pennies the white
boys threw at us to see if we were really monkeys
and would pick them up, the long bus ride home
to our side of things with people saying *nigger*

that September after Dr. King marched
to Washington, after our Sunday picnics in parks
where there seemed to be no war, the clouds
perfect rolls of baby blue and white through
the trees, over the crabs and chicken and pies

that autumn it began it seemed, the feelings
that were memories, the flying out of things,
soaring above the earth without my body,
a premature angel as I knew them, except
I was black in the mirrors, black of blackness

that left me dizzy on the playground, pennies
all around me, tap dancing to music from pain
shooting through me from the memories
of being used like a toy by faces now masks,
demons far more evil than little white boys.

Drowning

I have seen God face to face, and my life is preserved.
—Genesis 32:30

Held down underwater, fish meshing their eyes
to mine, the shout of the tide of water inside water
is all that this is not, this stinking sweat
of boy men, the stink of not having bathed, the smell
of what leaves the body gone dry and cracked and
then what is thrown in, as if the years ahead are nothing,
this earth I landed on is a false dream, a lie I chose
to make this bed hard, and the prayers are to some
beast that is turning all of us as my hands are held
by hands that should pull me up over the hardness
but makes the hardness a granite memory that will
always come back, and the hurt, *O God*, Jacob
must have said when he realized who the angel was,
awakening to swarms of flesh-eating fish
savoring blood, part human in ways we cannot see
walking on land, this karmic pain I will always
know as heartache until I learn love's lessons, as
if the gates to hell have my name engraved
in these waters, this sea where pain says . . . *remember.*

A Nightmare

The cinder block and chicken wire coldness
of isolation rooms, tile floors, the moon
waving in the glass, naked and unwrapped. I was
crouched like a bird to listen to the little voices
all around me, minute surreal whispers, gremlins
tiny and cute, except they carry wishes for me
to make my own breath crawl back inside me
and stop, for me to set my own rivers flowing
from my veins, so I am here in the hollow hands
of some strange caring, howling out ungodly
words that terrify me, some chanson we all knew
at home in heaven, as all I want is to go home,
although it is a sin to feed the lava stream of tears
my mother is crying at home, as if I cannot see her.

To Those Who Would Awaken

It will happen like this for many of you,
the house suddenly too much, the garden so full
you go out, maybe thinking of the way the earth gives
under your feet, the water making circles around them
if you have to cross a river, leaves and branches lift
up and then brushing against you when you have
crossed, these things or the very structure of things,
the making of the hip joint, electrical plots in the
heart, thalamus sending reminders to the moving,
you looking up into the still wings of gliding crows
on this day when you know in one second there
is the power to give things new names, so you decide
this is not leaving but returning, that ends are
middles or that there are no points, no time,
so by the time you are miles away from leaving
it is only the eternal very first moment of anything,
making a pound cake from scratch, moving your
hand across the hem of a new skirt, the slight fear
and tremble when a sudden sound hits your wall, like
children throwing the ball against the fire escape
until it rattles like an empty skeleton, the hot shower
where you are alone until the memories step
in with you, deep solitude of living alone, falling
to where you are connected with everything, and
it happens, the stepping out, mind full of seeing
yourself move out into the world without difference
so you can see every move you make is a change
in the current, the arrangement of patterns under a brush,
a twisted calligrapher's stroke, all these things, walking
while the bones of who you are become roots.

The One Song of He Nan Monastery

If I do not think of it, I do not hear it.
To hear it is to surrender to the chants,
their unchanging sound, the music
of the mountain. We tire and want to sit
or lie down along the way, but the words
insist that we move on, despite the fatigue,
the way the mind rises against itself.

It is a hammer made of silk, this music,
a soft commitment to one single point
in time, where all love ends, a history
of nothingness, a history of global war,
Earth folding its corners and baking us
in its own fire. It is a hammer made
of silk, these words no longer words.

I surrender to the smell of jasmine
when jasmine is anything but a flower.

Notes

The Government of Nature is the second book in a trilogy that began with *The Plum Flower Dance*.

The frontispiece is an original work written in Chinese by the author. Intended to be a verse to accompany his meditation, each line is a Chinese proverb using 心, the word for heart. Although no English translation has been done to date, it can be summarily taken as saying, "A quiet heart can be achieved with utter devotion and sincerity."

The translations of the Dao De Jing are by Jonathan Star.

The translation of Cold Mountain is by Red Pine.

The translation of the quote from Ying-an is by Thomas Cleary.

The park referred to in "In the Park with My Grandchildren" is named after Troy Bailey, an African American state senator whom Antero Pietila describes as having once been a pullman porter and union activist. Pietila, a longtime reporter for the Baltimore *Sun* and author of *Not in My Neighborhood* has written about the park, which was formally "Easterwood Park," in a time when that neighborhood was Jewish and working class.

The poem "Remember" was translated into Arabic by Wissal Al-Allaq for the Kalimah project in the United Arab Emirates. Ms. Allaq translated an entire collection by the author as a book entitled *Kama i' Reeh* (Like the Wind).

The dedication in "In Raleigh's Brownstone Hotel," is to Myrddin Wyltt (c. 540 to c. 584), who was a Welsh seer and prophet said to be one of the major personalities on which the wizard Merlin was based.

"Cold Mountain" refers both to the poet and a physical condition that occurs in certain states of meditation.

In referring to "the government of nature" (the book title and poem) the author makes reference to the Daoist idea that the internal human body is a microcosm of the outer world. References in drawings such as the *Tang Dynasty Internal Map* show the inner body as containing mountains, rivers, and so forth. It is said that there are inner and outer universes.

He Nan 和南寺 is a Buddhist temple and monastery on the eastern coast of Taiwan near the city of Hualien. He Nan Temple is where the author lived for a short time in the spring of 2005, at which time he wrote a series of poems that were the beginning of this collection.

Guan Yin is the Buddhist goddess of compassion. It is said that when she achieved Nirvana, she chose to sit at the gateway to heaven rather than enter so that she could help mortal beings find their way. A giant statue of her sits at the top of the hill in He Nan, facing the Pacific.

The characters adjacent to the cover illustration are from the opening of verse twenty-six of the *Dao De Jing*. The characters were translated by the late D. C. Lau as "The heavy is the root of the light / The still is the lord of the restless." These are also foundational concepts in Taijiquan.

The cover photo of giant cypress trees in Taiwan was taken by the author.

Acknowledgments

The author would like to thank the editors of the following publications for first publishing these poems, sometimes with other titles and in other versions:

American Poetry Review: "To Those Who Would Awaken," "Flying," "Elegy for the Appaloosa's Mother," "Scrapple," "The Ancestors Explain How Envy Grew," "At Lake Montebello with James," "Washing the Car with My Father," "For James"; *Artists and Influence*: "Against Forgiveness"; *Broom Review*: "Predators"; *Connotation Press*: "The Ancestors Speak to the Cowboy Uncle," "The Government of Nature"; *Green Mountains Review*: "With My Family at Dinner on Easter Sunday," "1963," "Petunias," "Christ Church, Oxford"; *Iron Horse*: "Drowning"; *New Letters*: "Interpretation of Tongues," "When My Heart Failed," "In Raleigh's Brownstone Hotel," "On Hearing Beethoven's 'Moonlight,'" "Looking Up from the Naked Bed"; *New Yorker*: "Passing through Indian Territory"; *Orion*: "Leaves"; *Poetry*: "The Ten Thousand"; *Poets & Writers*: "The Path"; *Poesis*: "Tsunami"; *Superstition Review*: "The Pantry," "If You Tell"; *Under the Rock Umbrella*: "A Dream of Emptiness"; *Washington Square*: "Weeping Willow," "Evening Lounge."

In Chinese culture one always gives respect to one's teacher, and so I express my deep and ongoing gratitude to Shiye Huang Chien Liang, who is the head of the Tien Shan Pai Association. I am one of his Dao disciples.

My life was changed when the Fulbright Association gave me an appointment to teach in Taiwan for the spring semester of 2002 as a Fulbright scholar at National Taiwan University (NTU) and Taipei National University of the Arts (TNUA).

During my time as a Fulbright scholar at NTU, Dr. Chinghsi Perng was my chairperson in theater, and he gave me my Chinese name. My friend Bei Ta in Beijing later suggested a slight modification in the name. Hsing Pen-ning, Andrew Pai, Bei Ta, Zang Di, Yu Jian, Wang Xiaoni, Mindy Zhang, Lin Melusine, Eric Mader,

Michelle Yeh, Yang Tze, Lu Ping Kwon, Zheng Chouyu, Yu Kwang-chung, Shi Zhi, and Maurus Young have all been of help to me.

Liu Zhigong and Alister Inglis were my first teachers when I took on two years of formal study of Mandarin at Simmons in 2002 with the college option of auditing courses for faculty members. Afterward, in my sabbatical year, 2004–2005, I lived in Taiwan for eight months and studied at Taipei Language Institute (TLI) under Teacher Lai, Teacher Feng, and Teacher Li. TLI was founded by Dr. Marvin Ho and is managed by Eleanor Chang.

Dr. Yu Hsi, director of He Han Temple and Monastery, gave me the space to live there for five weeks in the spring of 2005. At that time I wrote the poems that were the beginning of *The Government of Nature*, thus ending my seven year hiatus from my regular writing schedule.

Joan Houlihan of the Concord Poetry Center generously gave me invaluable advice and assistance in organizing the manuscript of this book.

Members of the recovery community and their supporters in various health fields who work to help survivors of childhood sexual abuse are of immense importance to everyone. Judith Herman and Mike Lew have made invaluable contributions, along with many other dedicated health care professionals.

My students at Simmons College have been indispensable in maintaining the nurturing atmosphere of the classroom that has helped my self-discovery. A teacher learns by teaching.

Friends from my childhood and adolescence have been loyal ever since, and there is not enough to say how much I appreciate them and their presence in my life.

Members of my immediate and extended family have given me loving support and believed in me in my difficult journey over the years. They are my root and foundation.